Union Public Library
1980 Morris Avenue
Union, N.J. 07

D1129764

People in My Community

Sanitation Worker

Union Public Library
1980 Morris Avenue
Union, N.J. 07083

by JoAnn Early Macken
Photographs by Gregg Andersen

Reading consultant: Susan Nations, M.Ed., author/literacy coach/consultant

WEEKLY (WR) READER®
EARLY LEARNING LIBRARY

Please visit our web site at: **www.earlyliteracy.cc**
For a free color catalog describing Weekly Reader® Early Learning Library's
list of high-quality books, call 1-877-445-5824 (USA) or 1-800-387-3178 (Canada).
Weekly Reader® Early Learning Library's fax: (414) 336-0164.

Library of Congress Cataloging-in-Publication Data

Macken, JoAnn Early, 1953-
    Sanitation worker / by JoAnn Early Macken.
       p. cm. — (People in my community)
    Summary: Photographs and simple text describe the work done by sanitation workers.
    Includes bibliographical references and index.
    ISBN 0-8368-3592-1 (lib. bdg.)
    ISBN 0-8368-3599-9 (softcover)
    1. Sanitation workers—Juvenile literature. 2. Refuse and refuse disposal—Juvenile literature.
    [1. Sanitation workers. 2. Occupations.] I. Title. II. Series.
    TD794.M33   2003
    628.4'42'092—dc21
                                               2002032776

First published in 2003 by
Weekly Reader® Early Learning Library
330 West Olive Street, Suite 100
Milwaukee, WI 53212 USA

Copyright © 2003 by Weekly Reader® Early Learning Library

Art direction: Tammy Gruenewald
Page layout: Katherine A. Goedheer
Photographer: Gregg Andersen
Editorial assistant: Diane Laska-Swanke

All rights reserved. No part of this book may be reproduced, stored in a retrieval system,
or transmitted in any form or by any means, electronic, mechanical, photocopying, recording,
or otherwise, without the prior written permission of the copyright holder.

Printed in the United States of America

1 2 3 4 5 6 7 8 9 07 06 05 04 03

Note to Educators and Parents

Reading is such an exciting adventure for young children! They are beginning to integrate their oral language skills with written language. To encourage children along the path to early literacy, books must be colorful, engaging, and interesting; they should invite the young reader to explore both the print and the pictures.

People in My Community is a new series designed to help children read about the world around them. In each book young readers will learn interesting facts about some familiar community helpers.

Each book is specially designed to support the young reader in the reading process. The familiar topics are appealing to young children and invite them to read — and re-read — again and again. The full-color photographs and enhanced text further support the student during the reading process.

In addition to serving as wonderful picture books in schools, libraries, homes, and other places where children learn to love reading, these books are specifically intended to be read within an instructional guided reading group. This small group setting allows beginning readers to work with a fluent adult model as they make meaning from the text. After children develop fluency with the text and content, the book can be read independently. Children and adults alike will find these books supportive, engaging, and fun!

— Susan Nations, M.Ed., author, literacy coach, and consultant in literacy development

Sanitation workers help keep a community clean. They pick up garbage and recyclables.

Sanitation workers carry heavy garbage cans. They lift heavy bags into a truck.

Sanitation workers drive big **garbage trucks**. They usually drive a different route each day of the week.

garbage truck

At the end of the day, they empty the truck. The garbage goes into a landfill or an incinerator.

Sanitation workers also drive street sweepers. The street sweepers pick up leaves and spray water on the streets to clean them.

Sanitation workers collect trash from parks. They pick up litter from streets and sidewalks.

They work in any kind of weather. Where it snows, they may drive **snowplows** in the winter.

snowplow

Trash belongs in a **trash can**. You don't litter, do you?

trash can

Glossary

incinerator — a furnace or container for burning garbage

landfill — a place where garbage is buried between layers of dirt

recyclables — objects like glass, plastic, and metal containers that can be treated or remade and used again

route — a line of travel

For More Information

Fiction Books

Rockwell, Anne F. *Career Day.*
  New York: HarperCollins Publishers, 2000.

Nonfiction Books

Bourgeois, Paulette. *Garbage Collectors.*
  Buffalo: Kids Can Press, 1998.

Deedrick, Tami. *Garbage Collectors.* Mankato,
  Minn.: Bridgestone Books, 1998.

Johnson, Jean. *Sanitation Workers, A to Z.*
  New York: Walker, 1988.

Maynard, Christopher. *Jobs People Do.*
  New York: DK Publishing, 2001.

Web Sites

What happens to your trash once you toss it?
www.kdhe.state.ks.us/kdsi/main_pg11.html
Waste management facts and resources from the Kansas
Department of Health and Environment

Index

community, 4
garbage, 4, 12
garbage bags, 6
garbage cans, 6
garbage trucks, 10
gloves, 8
incinerator, 12
landfill, 12

litter, 16, 20
recyclables, 4
route, 10
street sweepers, 14
snowplows, 18
trash, 16, 20
weather, 18

About the Author

JoAnn Early Macken is the author of children's poetry, two rhyming picture books, *Cats on Judy* and *Sing-Along Song,* and various other nonfiction series. She teaches children to write poetry and received the Barbara Juster Esbensen 2000 Poetry Teaching Award. JoAnn is a graduate of the MFA in Writing for Children Program at Vermont College. She lives in Wisconsin with her husband and their two sons.